INTRODUCTION

The Native North American Travelling College in Akwesasne has revised and updated our booklet, Traditional Mohawk Clothing. The original booklet was written by Tom Porter and Mike McDonald with illustrations by Brad Bonaparte and Tsionni Fox. New research into the material culture of the Mohawk, Haudenosaunee, and other indigenous nations has inspired us to take a closer look at the content of the original booklet to see where it could be enhanced. Our new edition is divided into two parts, historic and contemporary. The historic section shows the remarkable evolution that has occurred in the way we dressed over the centuries. It is illustrated with historic artwork found in museums, galleries, and old publications. The contemporary section presents traditional Mohawk clothing as it is worn in the Longhouse today.

Special thanks to Michael Galban of the Seneca Art and Culture Center at Ganondagan in Victor, New York for his kind assistance with the research and writing of the text of this booklet. Special thanks also to Carl Benn of Ryerson University for his help with the archival images of Native people of the northeast.

Darren Bonaparte, Mohawk historian and artist, wrote the accompaning text and assisted with the photo research. His work can be found at www.wampumchronicles.com.

Contemporary traditional clothing artists included in the publication include Marlana Thompson, Laura Thompson and Kawenniiosta Jock.

The staff at the Native North American Travelling College all made this booklet possible.

D1275941

Laura Thompson, women's contemporary outfit on this page and on the cover and back, Marlana Thompson.

Mohawk and Iroquoian clothing
1500s & 1600s

Before European contact, Mohawk clothing was made of animal hides like deer, moose, and caribou as well as fur-bearing animals like beaver, muskrat, raccoon and otter. The hides were tanned with the brains of the animal and smoked. Decoration was done with embroidery using moose hair, deer hair, or porcupine quills dyed in bright colors. Sometimes people painted designs on their clothing using natural earth pigments. Wampum beads and pendants cut from whelk and quahog shells as well as whole shells like the marginella were sometimes sewn onto garments to create beautiful contrasting patterns. The amount of clothing, of course, depended on the time of year.

Louis Nicholas, c.1678
Gilcrease Museum

Below the waist, men and women wore soft leather moccasins and leggings fitted nicely to the shape of the leg and coming up to the middle of the thigh. French explorer Jacques Cartier collected a pair of embroidered moccasins during one of his visits to the St. Lawrence River valley in the early 1500s. Men wore breechclouts which is a long strip of narrow leather that went between the man's legs with the ends going under and over a belt or sash tied around the waist. They were designed to fall halfway down the thigh and cut to cover mid-thigh to mid-thigh. Women wore wrap skirts made of leather that were also decorated.

Robes of animal fur and even netted blankets of bird feathers were worn anciently by both men and women. Large animals like bear, deer, elk and caribou were worn singly, but smaller animals like beaver, muskrat, raccoon and even chipmunks were cut into squares and sewn into rectangular robes which were often painted on the leather sides. They were worn with one shoulder exposed and held to the body by the other

Louis Nicholas, c.1678
Gilcrease Museum

hand or draped over both shoulders and sometimes belted at the waist. Woven fur robes of rabbit hide were also worn. These were made of twisted fur and woven into a net. These garments were lightweight and breathable—perfect for the cold winter nights.

Above the waist, men and women sometimes wore tunic-like shirts made from deerskin. It is also possible that an entire animal hide was draped over with an opening for their head to fit through like a poncho. They may have been stitched at the sides with sleeves that may or may not have been attached to the shirt at the shoulder. Any fringe edging on these early garments were very short nothing longer than a fingers width. Early European eye-witnesses left little information on clothing details of this early period. However, one thing that did get mentioned is that our men wore slatted wooden armor that might have been protection enough from war clubs but were no match for firearms.

Ornamentation like necklaces, bracelets and headbands—woven in shell beads like quahog, whelk and marginella—were common for both men and women. Women wore their hair long and plaited down the back. It was wrapped in beautiful, shiny eel skins. Bone combs with three or five teeth and simple bird and animal forms were worn by women tucked into the top of their queue. Red stone, shell, and slate gorgets were common for men to be worn at the neck. Flint knives hafted in wood handles were suspended around the neck as well.

Once native people became involved in the fur trade, European fabrics such as wool, cotton and linen became available. Wool, which is much easier to dry out than leather, soon became the material of choice for leggings, breech clouts, skirts, and wrap-around shawls and blankets. In essence, the old style of dress was retained but with a new materials to work in. Linen shirts that colonists wore were also popular with both males and females, as were hats and other item. Shoes and breeches or pants did not catch on right away. This resulted in a hybrid clothing style that reflected both cultures, European and Native, that persisted for centuries. Even colonial fur trader began to dress this way.

Hurons/Wendats, François Du Creux, Historiae Canadensis, 1664

Early-17th-century Hurons/Wendats
Samuel de Champlain, Voyages de
la Novvelle France, 1640

Louis Nicholas, c.1678
Gilcrease Museum

Louis Nicholas, c.1678
Gilcrease Museum

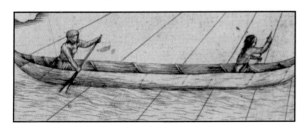

Hurons/Wendats in the 1600s
Nova Francia Acurata Delineatio,
1657, Toronto Public Library

Hurons/Wendats in the 1600s, Nova Francia Acurata Delineatio, 1657, Toronto Public Library

MOHAWK AND IROQUOIAN CLOTHING
1700s

The trend of hybrid native/colonial clothing continued through the 18th century. Increasing interaction with European traders meant more transfusion of culture going both ways.

Glass and ceramic beads of various sizes, shapes and colors were incorporated into the decoration of native clothing or were worn as necklaces. Native embroidery continued to be used as formerly but was also incorporated in the decoration of knife cases worn around the neck. Many examples of knife cases, pouches, and moccasins decorated with porcupine quills and glass beads from this era still exist in museums and galleries. They are also being reproduced by artisans today.

In the 18th century, metallic ornamentation became very popular among natives. This came in the form of arm bands, wrist bands, head bands, circular and crescent gorgets, and brooches and pins. Silver was prized by Mohawk people as it paralleled the use of bright white shell as a reflection of goodness and energy.

Historic art from this era depict our ancestors with this interesting mix of native and colonial styles and materials. There are also paintings of colonial officials such as Indian agents wearing a mix of native and colonial clothing.

Some native men who fought in the various colonial wars were sometimes made officers and given military coats and weaponry. These were worn and used even after the conflicts subsided. They must have created a very striking image.

Guy Johnson and David Hill – Karonghyontye, 1776
Benjamin West, National Gallery (U.S.)

Good Peter – Agwelon-dongwas, 1792 John Trumbull, Yale University

Mohawk woman with child – 18th century watercolor by unknown

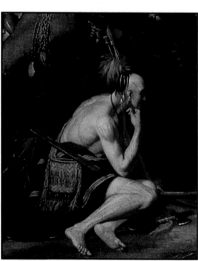

Death of Wolfe (detail), [1759]
Benjamin West, 1770
National Gallery of Canada

Four Indian Kings, 1710 John Verelst, Library and Archives Canada

Joseph Brant (Thayendanegea), 1776
George Romney, National Gallery of
Canada

Hendrick (Mohawk), c.1740
Anon., John Carter Brown Library

Mohawk 18th century
watercolor by
unknown

Cornplanter – Kiontwogky, 1796
F. Bartoli, New-York Historical Society

Mohawk and Iroquoian clothing
1800s

The 19th century saw a gradual change in clothing style among the Mohawk and other native nations in the Northeast woodlands.

The War of 1812 saw our native warriors dressing as they did in the 18th century, fighting in separate war parties in the native style. An artist who visited Akwesasne in the 1830s described our children as wearing nothing but breechclouts in the summer. Her watercolor paintings of adults show them wearing cloth shirts, skirts, leggings, and leather moccasins. An elderly woman is draped in a wool blanket. A man wears a blue trade shirt and sports silver bands around his arms and legs. He wears leather leggings, since pants had apparently not yet caught on among men. By the time of the American Civil War broke out in the early

Akwesasne on the St Lawrence River, 1838
Katherine Ellice, Library and Archives Canada

1860s, a shift had taken place. Native warriors no longer fought in separate war parties but were regular conscripts wearing uniforms like their non-native brethren.

Photographic images from the last half of the 19th century show that our people were dressing much more like people in the outside world, unless they were involved in a pursuit such as the selling of crafts or performing in various "wild west" shows popular at the time. The style of native clothing shows an enormous variety and complexity, and it is suggested that there was much more an influence of other tribes in this time period. Some native performers adopted the "Plains" style war bonnet, which non-native audiences had come to expect. Others wore a crown of long turkey feathers that was also popular at the time.

Circa 1890. The subjects are identified on the back as Seneca

Iroquois girl photographed in the late 1800s in Ontario, Canada

1870s albumen photograph of Solomon O'Bail (1814-1899), a Seneca and grandson of Cornplanter.

Daguerreotype of Caroline Parker, circa 1850.

circa 1852, daguerreotype portrait of an Iroquois man, probably Seneca,

Akwesasne on the St Lawrence River, 1838 Katherine Ellice, Library and Archives Canada

Iroquois, 1871

Thouhama or Sweetgrass, an Onondaga at Grand River, 1846 Henry Bowyer Lane, Library And Archives Canada

1849 of Seneca Iroquois, named Sos-heowa,

Circa 1860 tintype of two Seneca women in their traditional dress.

iroquois woman 1850's

cornelius krieghoff 1853 moccasin seller st.lawrence river

MOHAWK AND IROQUOIAN CLOTHING
EARLY TO MID 1900S

The 20th century demonstrates the continuing evolution of clothing styles here at Akwesasne and other native communities in the region. We must differentiate, of course, between the clothes our people wore in their day to day lives and that which they wore as performers or in ceremonies.

For everyday wear, native people wore whatever was available in stores or sewed what they needed. Photography shows them in non-native clothing with non-native hairstyles. Some ironworkers were known to look quite stylish because they had extra money due to their new professions. Less affluent folks back home were known to have at least one nice set of clothes to attend church and school. Thereare even photographs of people attending Longhouse ceremonies that show them wearing their best "non-native" clothing.

Seth Newhouse, Onondaga, early 1900's

in the 1930s and '40s. The Mohawk hairstyle—borrowed from 17th century Hurons—shows up a lot in this era, along with a version of leather leggings, moccasins, and vests seemingly patterned after the imagery of Hollywood cowboy movies.

In the latter half of the century, a new style emerged that was based on earlier clothing styles with the difference being in the proliferation of coloured and patterned cloth shirts, skirts, and leggings. These were adorned with coloured satin ribbons. In colonial times, the edges of skirts and leggings had silk ribbons sewn to them. The new ribbons also found their way to the shirts this time, decorating the chest, back, arms, shoulders and collars. Another evolution occurred with breech clouts, which were now more like a type of apron tied around the waist rather than the long strip of cloth of previous eras.

Native clothing continued to reflect the "anything goes" approach of the previous century, but it underwent another major transition that corresponded with the cultural revival taking place in our communities starting

The 20th century also saw the emergence of a standard form of headgear known as the kastoweh. This is a headdress based on a design from an earlier era. It features a narrow crown or band of either silver or leather and and array of turkey, partridge, and eagle feathers conform-

Akwesasne Mohawk Counselors Organization 1940.

Goldie Jamison Conklin, a Seneca, circa 1910

ing to Mohawk, Oneida, Onondaga, Cayuga, and Seneca conventions. It is not known when these particular feather arrangements originated, but they have become an essential part of traditional apparel today.

In the last decades of the 20th century, some of our people began to research and revive the style of native clothing from the colonial era. By studying written accounts in old books and archival documents, period artwork in museums and galleries, and surviving examples of clothing and accessories, these artisans are able to reproduce the stunning look of generations past. This has spilled over to hair styles, tattoos, piercings, and even the wearing of wampum or shell beads strung as necklaces or woven into collars and bands.

Native North American Travelling College travel troupe, 1974

Thomas Barnett Photographed in 1901

Condolers, Ohsweken, 1945

Sherman Smoke, Akwesasne Mohawk, 1950's

Iroquois in Buffalo, New York, 1914

Contemporary Haudenosaunee Clothing

Paintings by David Kanietakeron Fadden

Ribbon Shirts

Today this is the "minimum" of native apparel that you should have when attending ceremony or a social dance. While it is patterned after the colonial trade shirt, the addition of colored satin ribbons is a new innovation. Modern seamstresses are using their creativity to great effect when designing ribbon shirts.

BREECHCLOUTS

Breechclouts (sometimes called breech cloths) were once a long, rectangular strip of cloth or leather about five feet long and a foot wide. Today the breechclout looks like two wide, rectangular panels that are attached to each other at the top. They are worn around the waist with one flap in the front and other in the back, similar to the earlier form. These are decorated with ribbons, beadwork, and sometimes silver brooches. Some people wear normal pants beneath their breechclout whereas in the past the breechclout was worn on bare skin.

LEGGINGS

Although based loosely on the leggings of colonial times, modern examples vary in construction. Whereas leggings in the past had a flap that went on the outside of the leg, it is not uncommon in modern times to see them as more of a seam that faces the front of the leg with satin ribbons sewn on.

Skirts and Kilts

For women, the look and construction of skirts have not changed much. Some are still worn as a wraparound while others are sewn so that the edges meet. They usually match other elements of the clothing such as leggings and are embellished with ribbons, beadwork and silver brooches. Males sometimes wore kilts but these are rarely seen today.

Sashes and Garters

Some traditional outfits incorporate a sash worn around the waist. Some even wear a sash diagonally over one of the shoulders. These are often finger-woven from wool yarn or other materials. They may also have elaborate patterns of glass beads woven into them. It is also common for men to wear a pair of garters around the leg just below the knee. These can be finger-woven or made of leather with various items attached such as deer toes or bells.

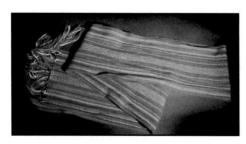

Yokes and Cuffs

Some traditional outfits have a yoke that covers the shoulders. This is sometimes made of velvet and has beaded decorations and edging. It is almost always separate from the actual shirt because you would remove it before tossing the shirt into the wash. The same would apply to the matching cuffs that go along with the outfit.

MOCCASINS

Moccasins were and still are part of the traditional Iroquoian dress. The Haudenosaunee had a moccasin that was made different from other nations. This particular moccasin had a single seam on its front. If a double seam was used it was very narrow almost appeared to be one seam. Other Iroquoian moccasins were very similar to other nations' way of making or designing them. The tanned and smoked hide of the moose was mostly used for making moccasins. The hide of a deer was also used, but not really favored. Moose hide was stronger, thicker, and much more durable. Moccasins were decorated with porcupine quills, moose hair and later with European seed beads.

There are basically four general types of moccasins. One is the boot type referred to as a mukluk. The second is the wrap around, the third is the regular low shoe type, and the fourth is the ankle height moccasin.

Today you will see a wide range of moccasin styles and decorations being worn to ceremony and social dances. While center seam moccasins do show up from time to time, you are more likely to see them with a wide vamp decorated with glass beads. It is not uncommon to see fur used in moccasin making, usually around the top edge where the foot slips in.

Women's Leather Moccasins

There really isn't much difference between the traditional footwear of men and women. Moccasins were and still are part of traditional apparel. In the pre-contact times, women put a raw hide buck skin (untanned) leather under the sole of the moccasin and then tied it together to make it last longer. They also did this because it protected the feet from anything hard or jagged they might walk on.

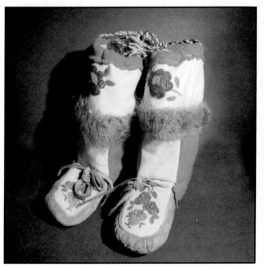

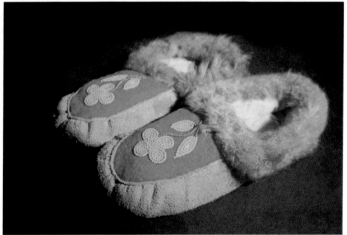

Kastowa

Mohawk headgear is known as the kastowa. It is identifiable by three upright eagle feathers. The rest of the feathers that decorate the kastowa are usually turkey feathers although some use the feathers of other birds like hawks and geese. Mohawks from Akwesasne have been known to incorporate the tail feathers of a partridge (or ruffed grouse) in their kastowa. The kastowa usually has a form made of black ash splints (the same material used in basketry) and a "crown" of some type that is made of a silver band or strip of leather. Some decorate this band with seed beads, tubular glass beads, or wampum. If it is the kastowa of a chief or Roiane, deer antlers are attached to the sides as a symbol of their office.

Roiane Kastowa

| Seneca | Cayuga | Onondaga | Oneida | Mohawk | Tuscarora |

Art by John Kahionhes Fadden

Accessories

No outfit would be complete without a few accessories. A leather tobacco and medicine pouch is commonly seen being worn to ceremony and in everyday life. These can be plain or fancy, depending on the owner's preference. Women often have purses or bags that sometimes match their clothing. Men and women may wear necklaces of various kinds. They are made with glass beads, wampum, and even bear claws. Some wear pendants and crescent-shaped gorgets reminiscent of the kind worn in colonial times. Silver and copper arm bands and wrist bands are also worn. Some men may carry a pipe or calumet as well as a war club or hatchet for use in the Smoke Dance. This is addition to the rattles, drums, and wooden sticks that are used in making music.

It should be noted that certain elements of contemporary traditional clothing are found in modern pow- wow regalia. Unfortunately, it is beyond the scope of this booklet to expand upon what is worn by pow-wow dancers today, but we will note that pow-wows held throughout the territories of the Haudenosaunee often feature Smoke Dance competitions in which more traditional clothing styles are worn and the music is our own.

Mantles and Shawls

Just like they did in historic times, women often wear mantles and shawls with their outfits. This is a piece of cloth that is wrapped around the shoulders. They sometimes have a fringe on the edges and may be decorated with ribbons and beadwork.

Symbols & Designs

The designs or symbols used to decorate clothing are made from nature and generally symbolize our dependence for survival on the life forms of all nature. They were usually composed of glass beads that were carefully and artfully stitched into the clothing, especially around the edges of leggings and skirts. Sky domes are very popular but people also include flowers, birds, and geometrical shapes like diamonds.

The first heart on this design represents a good minded person, the second heart is shaded representing grief, sorrow or death. The fern or fiddle head design between the hearts represents the vegetation of the earth.

The cycle of growth from the Mother Earth symbol.

The diagonal designs represent the fires(Councils or Governments) of different Nations, a united Nation.

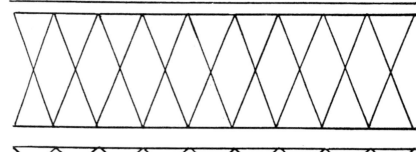

The net design represents a lacrosse net, snow shoe or a spider net.

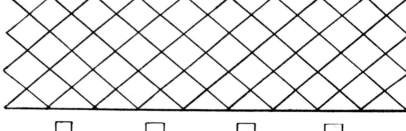

The holding hands or unity design comes from the Iroquois Wampum belts in this design each human symbol represents a nation or community.

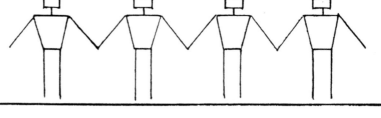

The waves of the water design.

In this design the half circles represent Sky Domes The straight line underneath the Sky Domes represents Mother Earth

Double Sky Dome

This particular design can have many different meanings although the Sky Domes and the Mother Earth remain the same, the cane shaped figure between the sky domes can represent corn or the Three Sisters (the Three Sisters being corn, beans and squash).

The mountain range design.

Double mountain range design.

VARIOUS BORDER DESIGNS USING BEAD AND APPLIQUE

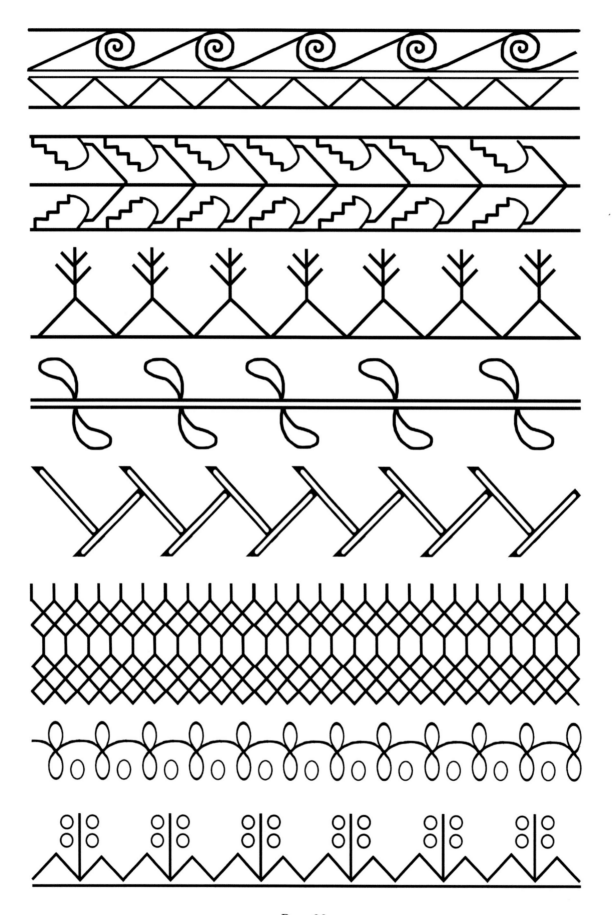

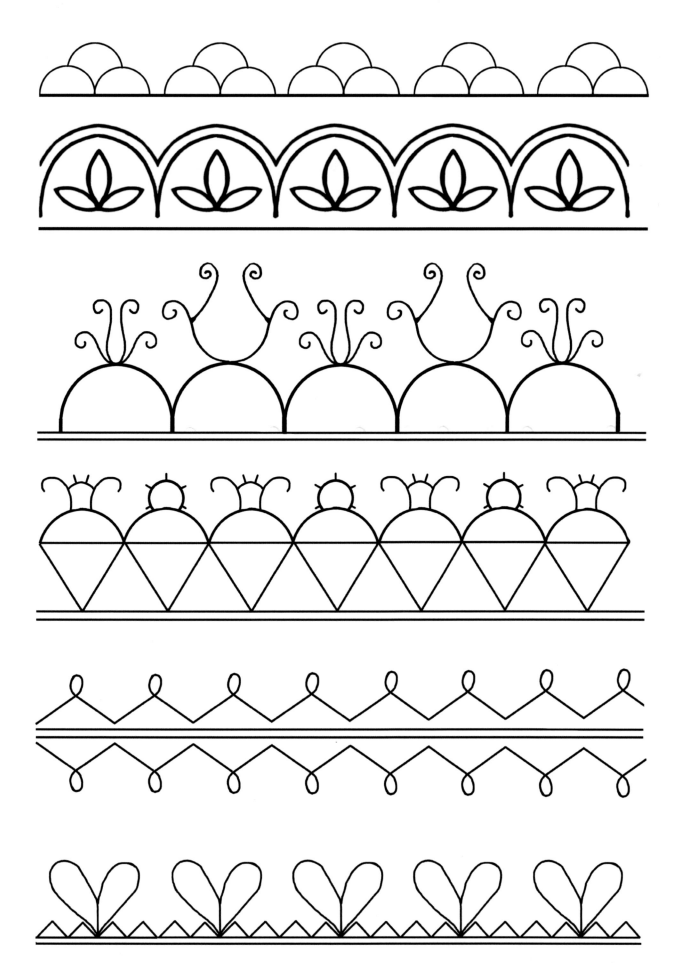

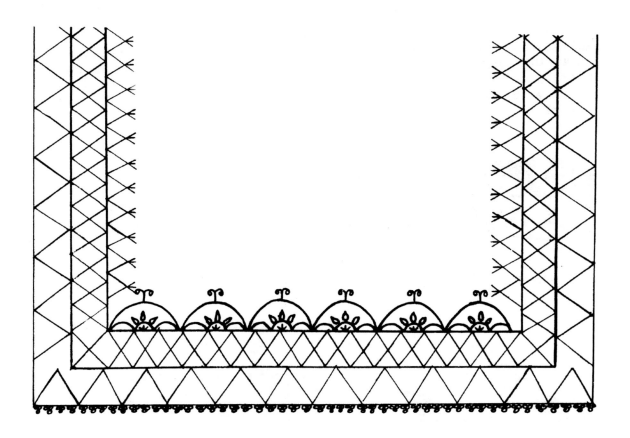

Border designs used for men's or women's leggings can be used for the aprons or breechclouts. It is very popular for the women's wraparound skirts.

The Native North American Travelling College has been at the forefront of cultural education and revitalization. It was established on the Akwesasne Mohawk Territory in 1974 under the name North American Indian Travelling College by Ernest Kaientaronkwen Benedict and Michael Kanentakeron Mitchell.

The Native North American Travelling College continues to evolve to meet the needs of a changing community. We need more than ever to promote and preserve our language culture and history, not only for our own sake, but to foster a greater appreciation and understanding in the outside community.

1 Ronathahon:ni Lane
Akwesasne, Ontario K6H 5R7

P.O. Box 273
Hogansburg, NY 13655

Tele: 613 932-9452
Fax: 613 932-0092
web: www.nnatc.org

Made in the USA
Middletown, DE
06 July 2022

68611529R00015